ISBN: 0-9826608-4-7
ISBN 13: 978-0-982-6608-4-3

You can visit us online at: *www.JacKrisPublishing.com*

Copyright 2011 by JacKris Publishing, LLC. All rights reserved. No part of this publication may be reproduced or transmitted in any form or by any means, electronic or mechanical, including photocopying, recording, or any information storage and/or retrieval system or device, without permission in writing from the publisher or as authorized by United States Copyright Law.

Printed in the United States of America.

Ver. 1.0.0-1

Second Semester

Copyright 2011. Winning With Writing Level 3 – Second Semester. All Rights Reserved.

# Preface

We have designed this thorough program to be user friendly for both teacher and student. This program is arranged in **36 weekly lessons**. Lessons 19 through 36 are contained in this Second Semester book. Lessons 1-18 are contained in the *Winning With Writing*, Level 3, First Semester book. Each lesson consists of five exercises labeled **Day 1** through **Day 5**.

Writing is very similar to other things in life; you need to have a plan and be well organized before you start. For example, you would never think of building a house without first having blueprints (plans) that clearly define the layout of the house. Without first having a plan, the house would certainly end up as a disconnected, unorganized mess.

In other words, you need to be organized before doing anything that is not obvious or simple. As I mentioned, being prepared before starting the actual drafting process is necessary. When writing we organize our writing by adhering to the following processes:

Outlining Process
1. The student first thinks of an idea (main topic) about which he wants to write.
2. The student then thinks of details that support his main topic. Instead of placing these details on a blank piece of paper, we provide a rough outline form when needed. This rough outline form is simply a place where general ideas are written in an organized manner. Completing the rough outline is the first step in organizing your writing.
3. After the student is through placing his ideas on the rough outline, it is used to build a final outline. It is during the transfer of information from the rough outline to the final outline that the details contained on the rough outline are further organized and developed into sentences for the actual writing assignment.

Drafting Process
1. The final outline is used as a guide to write a rough draft of the writing assignment. Typically, the student merely transfers the information contained on the final outline to the rough draft of the writing.
2. The student then edits the rough draft for grammar and content.
3. The final draft of the writing assignment is then written.

We believe this process is the easiest and most straight-forward way to write any type of writing. By using these processes, the difficult task of writing becomes extremely simple and easy for anyone. The processes taught in this book can be used for any type of writing of any length ranging from a single paragraph to an entire book.

Copyright 2011. Winning With Writing Level 3 – Second Semester. All Rights Reserved.

# Level 3 – Second Semester

## **Table of Contents**

Lesson 19 - Organizing and Writing a Paragraph .................................................................. 1

Lesson 20 - Transition Words and Time Order Words ......................................................... 14

Lesson 21 - Audience and Voice ........................................................................................... 23

Lesson 22 - Personal Narrative ............................................................................................. 29

Lesson 23 - Descriptive Paragraphs ..................................................................................... 38

   Lesson 24 - Review of Lessons 1-5 ................................................................................. 47

Lesson 25 - How-to Paragraphs ............................................................................................ 53

Lesson 26 - Persuasive Paragraphs ..................................................................................... 62

Lesson 27 - Informational Paragraphs .................................................................................. 71

Lesson 28 - Compare and Contrast Paragraphs .................................................................. 80

Lesson 29 - Writing Poems .................................................................................................... 89

   Lesson 30 - Review of Lessons 25-29 ............................................................................. 96

Lesson 31 - Friendly Letters ................................................................................................ 102

Lesson 32 - Book Reports ................................................................................................... 110

Lesson 33 - Short Reports .................................................................................................. 120

Lesson 34 - Biographies ...................................................................................................... 132

Lesson 35 - Short Stories .................................................................................................... 144

   Lesson 36 - Review of Lessons 31-35 ........................................................................... 153

Copyright 2011. Winning With Writing Level 3 – Second Semester. All Rights Reserved.

Student's Name: _Sophie_

# Winning With Writing Level 3

# Second Semester

Copyright 2011. Winning With Writing Level 3 – Second Semester. All Rights Reserved.

Lesson 19 Day 1

Date: _____

# Organizing and Writing a Paragraph

In this lesson you will write a paragraph by completing the writing process. So far when we have written we have not planned or arranged our thoughts. This was mainly because we were only writing one paragraph. It is fairly easy to draft one paragraph without creating an outline. But, what if we need to write multiple paragraphs? Back in Lesson 14 (in the First Semester book) we learned a little about the outlining process (which is a part of the **writing process**), but how do we actually write a paragraph by using this process? The writing process actually has two parts, the **outlining process** and the **drafting process**.

Here is an outline of the entire writing process.
- Outlining Process
    - Complete the rough outline
    - Complete the final outline
- Drafting Process
    - Complete the rough draft
    - Edit the rough draft
    - Complete the final draft

We will start the writing process by completing the **outlining process**.

Level 3, Lesson 19 – Organizing and Writing a Paragraph

Complete the rough outline

The outlining process starts by completing a rough outline. After the rough outline is complete, the information it contains will be used to develop a final outline. The final outline will then be used as a guide to write the rough draft of the paragraph.

Below is a sample rough outline that shows its parts:

Rough Outline

- Main Topic
    - Detail #1: (used to make detail sentences
    - Detail #2: in the final outline)
    - Detail #3:

May be more or fewer than three

*Step #1 (develop a main topic)*

The first piece of information needed to complete the rough outline is a **main topic**. A main topic is a **very general idea** that tells what a paragraph is about. For example, let's assume we have decided that we want to write a paragraph about **making homemade pizza**. This would be the **main topic** of our paragraph. A main topic does not need to be a complete sentence; it is a very general **idea** for your paragraph.

A. Think of a main topic for your paragraph. You can write about **the biggest surprise you've ever had**, **your dream vacation**, or choose **a main topic of your own**. Write it in the **main topic** section of your rough outline at the end of today's lesson.

*Step #2* (develop details)

Now that we have a main topic (the sample is **making homemade pizza**), we need to think of **details** to complete the rough outline. A detail can be a thought, phrase, or sentence that gives more information about the main topic. These details will be turned into **detail sentences** for the **final outline**.

Assume we possess no knowledge of our example main topic **how to make homemade pizza**, so we conduct some research to gather information from the library, Internet, and other dependable sources. Our research returns the following general **details** about making homemade pizza:

1. make sauce for the pizza
2. prepare toppings
3. make the dough

These are **details** because they provide more description of the main topic.

B. Think of a few details for your main topic and write them under the **details** section of the rough outline. With the addition of your **details**, the rough outline is complete.

# Rough Outline

Main Topic:

Detail #1:

Detail #2:

Detail #3:

**Lesson 19 Day 2**

Date: _____

# Organizing and Writing a Paragraph

Our completed sample rough outline from Day 1 looks like this:

**Rough Outline**

**Main Topic**: making homemade pizza

**Detail #1**: make sauce for the pizza

**Detail #2**: prepare toppings

**Detail #3**: make the dough

We will now continue the outlining process by using the information in the rough outline to create the final outline.

Complete the final outline

A final outline for a single paragraph has the following structure:

- Topic sentence:
- Detail Sentence #1: (constructed from the main
- Detail Sentence #2: topic and details in the
- Detail Sentence #3: rough outline)   *(May be more or fewer than three)*
- Ending sentence:
    (restates the topic sentence and/or summarizes the detail sentences)

*Step #1* (write a topic sentence)

The first step to completing a final outline is writing a **topic sentence**. A topic sentence tells **generally** what the paragraph is about, but it does not provide specific detail about the paragraph. Its primary purpose is to get the attention of the reader.

By looking at the **main topic** and **details** written on the rough outline, we can use them to think of a **topic sentence** for the final outline. While the main topic on the rough outline may or may not be a complete sentence, the topic sentence on the final outline **must** be a complete sentence. Using our example main topic of **making homemade pizza**, our topic sentence could be something like the following sentence: **It is fun to make homemade pizza**.

A. Write a topic sentence for your main topic on the final outline at the end of today's lesson.

*Step #2* (writing detail sentences)

The next piece of information needed to build the final outline is detail sentences. Detail sentences will make up the greatest portion of your writing because they actually tell the story. This makes the detail sentences the most important part of the writing.

Look at the **details** written on the rough outline. It is our goal to use these **details** along with the **main topic** and **topic sentence** to think of interesting detail sentences for the final outline. While you are thinking of these **detail sentences**, remember that they will all need to fit together as a paragraph. By the time you are done you should have several detail sentences written under the **detail sentences** section of the final outline. Make sure to place the detail sentences in the correct order if there is a required order for your writing.

B. Since you now have all of the information you need to think of detail sentences for your paragraph, write your detail sentences in the detail sentences section of the final outline which is located at the end of today's lesson.

After looking at our details, main topic, and topic sentence from our example (making homemade pizza), we added some detail sentences to our final outline. Our final outline now looks like this:

## Final Outline

Topic Sentence:

   It is fun to make homemade pizza.

Detail Sentences:

- The sauce for the pizza contains a bit of garlic.
- Use pepperoni and cheese, and spread it on thick.
- The dough can be tricky to make, so be sure to add plenty of yeast.

Ending Sentence:

   (not developed yet)

*Step #3* (writing an ending sentence)

The last step to completing the final outline is creating an **ending sentence**. It is the function of the ending sentence to restate the topic sentence or summarize the detail sentences. For our example above, we could write the following ending sentence:

> "Making homemade pizza is fun because you are actually making something delicious from simple ingredients."

C. Create an ending sentence for your paragraph and write it on the **ending sentence** section of your final outline. With the addition of the ending sentence, your final outline is complete.

# Final Outline

**Topic Sentence:**

**Detail Sentence #1:**

**Detail Sentence #2:**

**Detail Sentence #3:**

**Ending Sentence:**

Lesson 19 Day 3

Date: _____

# Organizing and Writing a Paragraph

Now that we have completed the outlining process, it is time to move on to the **drafting process**. The drafting process is where we use the information contained in the final outline to complete a rough draft of our paragraph, edit the rough draft, and complete a final draft of our paragraph.

Complete the Rough Draft

So far you have spent quite a bit of time filling out the rough outline and the final outline. As a result, your final outline has all of the necessary pieces to complete a rough draft of your paragraph.

If you think of something you want to add while you are writing your rough draft, please do so. The final outline will now be used as a guide to write a rough draft.

Start by writing your **topic sentence** on the lines below. Next, write the **detail sentences** in the order in which they occur in your final outline. Finish your paragraph with the **ending sentence**.

_____
_____
_____
_____
_____
_____
_____
_____

Level 3, Lesson 19 – Organizing and Writing a Paragraph

**Lesson 19 Day 4**

Date: _____

# Organizing and Writing a Paragraph

<u>Edit the rough draft</u>

It is now time to **edit** the rough draft you wrote on Day 3. Does your paragraph say what you want it to say? Do your sentences make sense? Are they in the correct order?

Also, look for and fix the following errors:

1) incorrectly used, misspelled, or misplaced words,

2) incorrect or missing spacing,

3) incorrect, missing, or misplaced punctuation, and

4) incorrect or missing capitalization.

**Lesson 19 Day 5**

# Organizing and Writing a Paragraph

Date: _____

## Complete the Final Draft

On Day 4 you edited your rough draft paragraph. Today you will rewrite your paragraph in its final draft form.

Read your paragraph one more time. Do your sentences flow well from one to the other? Does your entire paragraph make sense? Can you make it even better by adding **strong verbs** and **adverbs**? Rewrite your edited paragraph below.

_____
_____
_____
_____
_____
_____
_____
_____
_____
_____
_____
_____
_____
_____

Level 3, Lesson 19 – Organizing and Writing a Paragraph

**Lesson 20 Day 1**

Date: _____

# Transition Words and Time Order Words

In Lesson 16 we learned to use the words **first**, **second**, **next**, **later**, **then**, and **finally** to introduce our sentences when a story needs to be told in a specific order. These words are called **time order transition words**. There are also other words that are transition words that are not necessarily **time order** related.

A sample of other transition words are **before**, **now**, **after**, **one day**, **also**, **sometimes**, **now**, **since**, **however**, **at last**, **once**, and **even though**. These words are used to make paragraphs **flow** better even when the story does **not** need to be told in a specific time order.

What does **flow better** mean? We will use the following two paragraphs to explain.

Once upon a time there were three little pigs. They were scared of the big bad wolf. He kept saying that he would blow their old house down. The three little pigs decided to build their own stronger houses. The first little pig built his house out of straw. The second little pig decided to build his house out of sticks. The last little pig decided to build his house out of bricks. The wolf was able to blow down the houses that were made of straw and sticks. He was unable to blow down the house made of bricks.

Level 3, Lesson 20 – Transition Words and Time Order Words

Once upon a time there were three little pigs. They were scared of the big bad wolf since he kept saying that he would blow their old house down. First, the three little pigs decided to build their own stronger houses. Next, the first little pig built his house out of straw. Then, the second little pig decided to build his house out of sticks. At last, the last little pig decided to build his house out of bricks. The wolf was able to blow down the houses that were made or straw and sticks. However, he was unable to blow down the house made of bricks.

Can you see how the second paragraph flows better than the first? By using time order transition words and other transition words, the second paragraph does not seem quite as choppy as the first paragraph. The time order transition words also give some order to the paragraph by using words like **first**, **next**, **however**, and **finally**.

A. Go back and underline all of the **transition words** that were added to the second paragraph.

**Lesson 20 Day 2**

Date: _____

# Transition Words and Time Order Words

A. Here is another paragraph that does not contain any transition words. Add a "∧" symbol (**caret** symbol) where you would like to insert a transition word. Write the word you are adding above the **caret**. Use the words in the box as transition words for the paragraph below.

| first | then | sometimes | once | even though |

In the summer we like to eat our dessert outside. We eat our dinner inside the house. We eat our dessert on the patio. We eat watermelon for dessert. We had homemade ice cream. We had a big watermelon last night. My uncle still brought over an apple pie for us to eat for dessert. It's always nice to have a choice of desserts.

B. Rewrite the above paragraph with the **transition words** included.

_____
_____
_____
_____
_____
_____
_____
_____
_____
_____

Level 3, Lesson 20 – Transition Words and Time Order Words

**Lesson 20 Day 3**

# Transition Words and Time Order Words

Date: _____

A. Transition words are usually words that tell **when**. So far we have listed the following transition words: **before**, **now**, **after**, **one day**, **also**, **sometimes**, **since**, **however**, **at last**, **once**, and **even though**.

Can you think of three other **transition words** that could tell when?

1. _____

2. _____

3. _____

**Lesson 20 Day 4**

# Transition Words and Time Order Words

Date: _____

Below is a paragraph from Lesson 16 (First Semester) that tells a short story about getting a drink of water. The **time order transition words** have been bolded.

There is nothing like a cold glass of water to satisfy my thirst. **First**, I get a clean glass from the cabinet. **Next**, I remove the pitcher of ice water from the refrigerator. **Then**, I put ice cubes into my empty glass. **Finally**, I fill my glass with water. There is nothing like a cool glass of water.

Below is the same paragraph rewritten to include **time order transition words** and other **transition words**.

There is nothing like a cold glass of water to satisfy my thirst. **Soon** after I get home, I get a clean glass from the cabinet. **Then**, I remove the pitcher of ice water from the refrigerator. **During** that time I put ice cubes into my empty glass. **At last**, I fill my glass with water. **Later**, I may have another glass because there is nothing like a cool glass of water.

You can see how adding other **transition words** makes the second paragraph more interesting. The paragraph as originally written sounds more like a step by step recipe for making a glass of ice water than it does a short story about making a glass of water.

Level 3, Lesson 20 – Transition Words and Time Order Words

A. The paragraph below does not contain any **transition words**. Insert the appropriate **transition words** from the box onto each line. Remember to use correct punctuation when necessary.

| as soon as | soon | later | during |

1. _____ the summer I like to have a lemonade stand where I sell fresh lemonade. 2. _____ after I get my stand set up, people come to buy! 3. _____ my pitcher is out of the lemonade, I take my stand down and go back inside the house. 4. _____, I take some time to count the money I made during the day.

Lesson 20
Day 5

# Transition Words and Time Order Words

Date: _____

A. Arrange the following sentences into a paragraph. Add **transition words** from the box to each sentence.

> as soon as   today   initially   later   eventually

1. I removed one of my favorite books from the shelf.
2. I opened the book, I began to read.
3. My eyes got tired and I had to stop reading.
4. My eyes felt better, I started to read again for a little longer.
5. That night I finished the entire book.

Level 3, Lesson 20 – Transition Words and Time Order Words

**Lesson 21 Day 1**

Date: _____

# Audience and Voice

In Lesson 11 (First Semester) we learned about using formal and informal language. During that lesson you learned to consider your audience when deciding what kind of language to use. This lesson will talk a bit more about different **voices** and **audiences**.

When we get ready to write something, we should first determine who our intended audience will be. Also, what message are we trying to deliver to our audience? Here are some more things to consider.

- Are you trying to make friends with your audience?
- Are you trying to be funny?
- Are you upset and need to show your anger?
- Are you trying to write a business communication?
- Are you simply trying to express your point of view?
- Are you trying to convince your audience to agree with you?
- Do you care if you make your audience angry?
- Is the intended audience familiar with your topic, or do you need to explain it to them by using simpler words?

Depending on the message you are trying to send, you will use an **angry**, **happy**, **sad**, **funny**, **friendly**, or **business** voice.

A. Choose from the **voices** in the box below. Write on each line the type of voice you would use for each writing.

| friendly | angry | happy |
|----------|-------|-------|
| business | sad   | funny |

1. _____ a letter complaining about an unfair parking ticket

2. _____ a quick thank you note to one of your friends

3. _____ a letter to Grandma informing her that your favorite fish has just died

4. _____ a letter to one of your best friends telling them about something funny you did

5. _____ a letter to a business about returning a new shirt that you bought that does not fit

6. _____ a joke you have written to one of your friends

Level 3, Lesson 21 – Audience and Voice

Lesson 21 Day 2

# Audience and Voice

Date: _____

Once you choose the voice for your writing, make sure you stick to that voice for the entire writing, especially if it is a shorter writing.

A. Read the following note. Do you see anything wrong with it? Write an **X** next the correct answer below.

To whom it may concern,

My name is Dora and I am writing to let you know how very upset I am with your store. The last time I was in your store I was treated very rudely. The cashier made me wait forever before he finally helped me. I do not think I will ever come back into your store. Of course while I was there I did see some really cool shoes that I might need to purchase sometime. They are a pretty shade of blue and have sparkles. Do you have them in a size 6?

Sincerely,

Ima Knothapy


1. ___ This note doesn't make sense because it is a complaint.

2. ___ This note contains two different voices, angry and happy.

3. ___ The writer did not know the maker of the shoes.

4. ___ The writer did not tell the truth about coming back to the store.

Level 3, Lesson 21 – Audience and Voice

**Lesson 21 Day 3**

## Audience and Voice

Date: _____

A. If you were to write the following types of writings, what type of **audience** would you expect to attract? Write the answers from the box on the lines below.

| yourself | children | adults | people in the public |
|----------|----------|--------|----------------------|
| teenagers | family members | friends | parents |

1. _____ an entry in your diary

2. _____ a story about a cartoon you saw

3. _____ an advertisement for a play

4. _____ an invitation to a family reunion

5. _____ a story about skateboarding

6. _____ an article about how a computer chip operates

7. _____ an invitation to your birthday party

8. _____ a letter asking if your allowance can be increased

Level 3, Lesson 21 – Audience and Voice

**Lesson 21 Day 4**

Date: _____

## Audience and Voice

A. Write a one paragraph story about something that made you **sad** or **unhappy** during the past week. Make sure to use a **sad** or **slightly angry voice** for your paragraph. Remember to use correct paragraph form.

Level 3, Lesson 21 – Audience and Voice

**Lesson 21 Day 5**

Date: _____

## Audience and Voice

A. Write a one paragraph story about something fun you did during the past week. Use a **funny** or **happy voice** for your paragraph. Remember to use correct paragraph form.

**Lesson 22 Day 1**

Date: _____

# Personal Narrative

In this lesson you will write a one paragraph **personal narrative**. A personal narrative is a **true story** about something that happened to **you** or **something you did**. It does not have to be a story about something fantastic or larger than life. A good narrative can be about something very simple.

Why do people write personal narratives? Some people write them simply because they want to share an experience. Sometimes they write them to entertain the reader. Personal narratives can be happy, scary, sad, or any feeling in between.

Audiences for a personal narrative can range from a friend, a parent, or even a teacher. The writer needs to keep his audience in mind as he chooses his words.

Develop and write a personal narrative using the following writing process:

Outlining Process
   A. Choose a main topic
   B. Complete the rough outline
   C. Complete the final outline

Drafting Process
   A. Complete the rough draft
   B. Edit the rough draft
   C. Complete the final draft

**Outlining Process**

We will now begin writing a personal narrative with the outlining process. Outlining is the process where information about the writing is gathered in order to complete a rough outline and a final outline.

Choose a main topic

Write about one of the following:
- a game you like to play
- something nice you did for someone
- a time when you worked so hard you got really tired

Choose your main topic and write it in the main topic section of the rough outline.

The entire outlining process is explained in **Appendix A**. If you need help in completing the rough outline or the final outline, use Appendix A. Whether or not you use Appendix A, you still need to complete the rough outline and the final outline on the next two pages of this lesson.

## Complete the rough outline

### Rough Outline

**Main topic:** _____

**Detail #1:** _____

**Detail #2:** _____

**Detail #3:** _____

**Lesson 22 Day 2**

Date: _____

# Personal Narrative

Complete the final outline

Final Outline

**Topic sentence:**
_____
_____
_____
_____

**Detail sentence #1:**
_____
_____
_____
_____

**Detail sentence #2:**
_____
_____
_____
_____

**Detail sentence #3:**
_____
_____
_____
_____

**Ending sentence:**
_____
_____
_____
_____

Level 3, Lesson 22 – Personal Narrative

Lesson 22
Day 3

Date: _____

# Personal Narrative

## Drafting Process

### Complete the rough draft

So far you have spent quite a bit of time filling out the rough outline and the final outline. As a result, your final outline has all of the necessary pieces to complete your writing.

If you think of something you want to add while you are writing your rough draft, please do so. The final outline will now be used as a guide to write a rough draft of the writing.

Start by writing your **topic sentence**, **detail sentences**, and **ending sentence** on the lines below.

_____
_____
_____
_____
_____
_____
_____
_____
_____
_____
_____
_____
_____
_____

Level 3, Lesson 22 – Personal Narrative

**Lesson 22 Day 4**

Date: _____

## Personal Narrative

### Edit the rough draft

It is now time to **edit** the rough draft you wrote on Day 3. Does your paragraph say what you want it to say? Do the words you chose make sense?

Look for and fix the following errors: 1) incorrectly used, misspelled, or misplaced words, 2) incorrect or missing spacing, 3) incorrect, missing, or misplaced punctuation, and 4) incorrect or missing capitalization.

**Lesson 22 Day 5**

Date: _____

# Personal Narrative

<u>Complete the final draft</u>

On Day 4 you edited your paragraph. Today you will rewrite your paragraph in its final draft form.

Read your paragraph one more time. Do your sentences make sense? Are your sentences related enough to be in the same paragraph? Can you make it even better by adding 1) **transition words**, 2) **strong verbs**, 3) **adverbs**, 4) **exact nouns**, or 5) **descriptive adjectives**? Rewrite your edited paragraph below in its final form.

Level 3, Lesson 22 – Personal Narrative

**Lesson 23 Day 1**

Date: _____

# Descriptive Paragraphs

In this lesson you will write a one paragraph **descriptive paragraph**. A descriptive paragraph tells about a person, place, or thing. The goal of a good descriptive paragraph is to involve the reader in the story as much as possible. You want the reader to feel like they were actually there during the events of the story.

In order to bring the reader into the story, it is necessary to use exciting adjectives. Here is an example of a descriptive paragraph.

### My Trip to the Cookie Factory

I like going on field trips, especially to places that have tasty things to eat. We recently went to the Kooky Llama Cookie Factory. Immediately upon entering the large building, the aroma of freshly baked chocolate chip cookies filled the warm air. We were soon led into an area where cookies were being baked. Before entering this area we had to put on long protective jackets designed to prevent us from spreading contaminates on the cookies. In this area people were wearing round hats and brightly colored uniforms. They were rushing around doing things like mixing fresh ingredients for cookie dough and packaging the warm, freshly baked cookies. This area was so clean you could have eaten off of the floor. Finally, as my stomach was starting to growl from smelling the freshly baked cookies, we were taken into a room where we were told we could eat all of the cookies that we wanted. There were several flavors from which to choose. I was full by the time we left the factory. This field trip was truly one of my favorites!

Level 3, Lesson 23 – Descriptive Paragraphs

Develop and write a descriptive paragraph using the following writing process:

Outlining Process
   A. Choose a main topic
   B. Complete the rough outline
   C. Complete the final outline

Drafting Process
   A. Complete the rough draft
   B. Edit the rough draft
   C. Complete the final draft

**Outlining Process**

We will now begin writing a descriptive paragraph with the outlining process. Outlining is the process where information about the writing is gathered in order to complete a rough outline and a final outline.

Choose from one of the following main topics:

- your favorite restaurant
- a person whom you admire
- a favorite piece of art

Write your main topic in the main topic section of the rough outline.

The entire outlining process is explained in **Appendix A**. If you need help in completing the rough outline or the final outline, use Appendix A. Whether or not you use Appendix A, you still need to complete the rough outline and the final outline on the next two pages of this lesson.

## Complete the rough outline

## Rough Outline

**Main topic:** _____

**Detail #1:** _____

**Detail #2:** _____

**Detail #3:** _____

**Lesson 23 Day 2**

Date: _____

# Descriptive Paragraphs

Complete the final outline

Final Outline

**Topic sentence:**
_____
_____
_____
_____
_____

**Detail sentence #1:**
_____
_____
_____
_____
_____

**Detail sentence #2:**
_____
_____
_____
_____
_____

**Detail sentence #3:**
_____
_____
_____
_____
_____

**Ending sentence:**
_____
_____
_____
_____
_____

**Lesson 23 Day 3**

Date: _____

# Descriptive Paragraphs

## Drafting Process

<u>Completing the rough draft</u>

So far you have spent quite a bit of time filling out the rough outline and the final outline. As a result, your final outline has all of the necessary pieces to complete your writing.

If you think of something you want to add while you are writing your rough draft, please do so. The final outline will now be used as a guide to write a rough draft of the writing.

Start by writing your **topic sentence**, **detail sentences**, and **ending sentence** on the lines below.

_____
_____
_____
_____
_____
_____
_____
_____
_____
_____

Level 3, Lesson 23 – Descriptive Paragraphs

**Lesson 23 Day 4**

Date: _____

# Descriptive Paragraphs

## Edit the rough draft

It is now time to **edit** the rough draft you wrote on Day 3. Does your paragraph say what you want it to say? Do the words you chose make sense?

Look for and fix the following errors: 1) incorrectly used, misspelled, or misplaced words, 2) incorrect or missing spacing, 3) incorrect, missing, or misplaced punctuation, and 4) incorrect or missing capitalization.

**Lesson 23 Day 5**

Date: _____

# Descriptive Paragraphs

Complete the final draft

On Day 4 you edited your paragraph. Today you will rewrite your paragraph in its final draft form.

Read your paragraph one more time. Do your sentences make sense? Are your sentences related enough to be in the same paragraph? Can you make it even better by adding 1) **transition words**, 2) **strong verbs**, 3) **adverbs**, 4) **exact nouns**, or 5) **descriptive adjectives**? Rewrite your edited paragraph below in its final form.

Level 3, Lesson 23 – Descriptive Paragraphs

*Lesson 24 Review Day 1*

Date: _____

# Review of Organizing and Writing a Paragraph

Below you will see a list of steps necessary to **make a sandwich**. Put them in the order they must be performed by placing the numbers **1 - 3** next to them. Also add two **details** for each **subtopic**.

1. <u>making a sandwich</u>

___
......

a.____ spread condiments on the bread

_____
-------------------------------------------------------------------
_____
-------------------------------------------------------------------
_____

___
......

b.____ get two pieces of bread

_____
-------------------------------------------------------------------
_____
-------------------------------------------------------------------
_____

___
......

c.____ add meat and cheese

_____
-------------------------------------------------------------------
_____
-------------------------------------------------------------------
_____

Level 3, Lesson 24 - Review of Lessons 19-23

**Lesson 24 Review Day 2**

Date: _____

# Review of Transition Words and Time Order Words

A. The paragraph below does not contain any **transition words**. Insert the appropriate **transition words** from the box onto each line.

| at last | soon | when | also | first | one time |

1. _____ it starts raining in the spring, Dad and I know what that means. 2. _____ it will be time to get the lawnmower out for another busy season. 3. _____, we make sure that the lawnmower is full of gas and that it will start after sitting all winter. 4. _____, Dad checks the cutting blade to make sure it is sharp enough to cut grass. 5. _____ Dad had to remove the blade and sharpen it with a grinder to give it a nice sharp edge. 6. _____, it is time to get the mower out and cut the lawn. Summer is finally here.

Level 3, Lesson 24 - Review of Lessons 19-23

**Lesson 24 Review Day 3**

Date: _____

# Review of Audience and Voice

A. If you were to write the following things, what type of audience would you expect to attract? Write the answers from the box on the lines below.

| yourself | children | adults | people in the public |
| teenagers | co-worker | friends | parents |

1. _____ a grocery list for your Mom or Dad

2. _____ a note to remind yourself of something

3. _____ a story about the newest video game

4. _____ a letter about your boss

5. _____ a blog entry for people who like you

6. _____ an advertisement for an opera in your town

7. _____ a how-to article giving step-by-step instructions how to file Federal taxes

8. _____ a story about a little train that could do anything if he put his mind to it

Level 3, Lesson 24 - Review of Lessons 19-23

Lesson 24 Review Day 4

Date: _____

# Review of a Personal Narrative

A. Below are the steps one must take to write a **personal narrative**. Place them in the correct order by placing the numbers **1 - 7** on the lines below.

1. ____ Select details for your story.

2. ____ Decide on a topic.

3. ____ After your story makes sense, add strong verbs and exciting adjectives as you write your final draft.

4. ____ Add a topic sentence and an ending sentence right before you write your rough draft.

5. ____ Write a rough draft of your story.

6. ____ Check to make sure your story makes sense as written in a rough draft.

7. ____ Check for proper punctuation and capitalization and rewrite the story in its final form.

Level 3, Lesson 24 - Review of Lessons 19-23

**Lesson 24 Review Day 5**

# Review of Descriptive Paragraphs

Date: _____

A. The paragraph below is pretty boring since it does not contain many descriptive words. Add your own descriptive words that describe things related to **smell**, **hearing**, **sight**, **taste**, and **touch**. Change the sentences as necessary in order for your words to fit and make sense.

   I like to play games with my friends. Once we played a game with a game board that was colorful. It had many pieces and money. Sometimes we play games in our yard. My friend is a runner and usually wins races. We also like to kick a ball to each other.

Level 3, Lesson 24 - Review of Lessons 19-23

**Lesson 25 Day 1**

# How-to Paragraphs

Date: _____

In this lesson you will write a one page **how-to paragraph**. A how-to paragraph tells the reader how to complete one task. A typical how-to paragraph starts by telling the reader what materials, if any, are needed to accomplish the task. The remaining portion of a how-to paragraph explains the steps necessary to complete the task.

A how-to paragraph is different from a personal narrative or descriptive paragraph in that it does **not** focus on making the paragraph more interesting by adding descriptive words. Instead, a **how-to paragraph** only gives information necessary for the reader to understand what needs to be done. Here is an example of a how-to paragraph.

## How to Help Mom with the Laundry

Once in a while Mom asks me to help her with the laundry. To do this, I need some laundry detergent, softener, and anti-static dryer sheets. First, the laundry must be separated into different piles of colored and white laundry. If the colored laundry is not separated from the white laundry, I might end up with white laundry that is not white anymore. Next, I load one of the piles of dirty laundry into the washer. I pour laundry detergent and fabric softener into the washer. Then, I close the door and start the washer. Sometime later, after the wash cycle has completed, the clean laundry is removed from the washer and loaded into the dryer. An anti-static dryer sheet is placed in the dryer along with the wet laundry, and the dryer is then started. After the dryer cycle is complete, the clothes are removed from the dryer and folded. I do not mind helping Mom because it is fun and gives her more time to spend with me.

Level 3, Lesson 25 – How-to Paragraphs

Develop and write a how-to paragraph using the following writing process:

Outlining Process
   A. Choose a main topic
   B. Complete the rough outline
   C. Complete the final outline

Drafting process
   A. Complete the rough draft
   B. Edit the rough draft
   C. Complete the final draft

## **Outlining Process**

We will now begin writing a how-to paragraph with the outlining process. Outlining is the process where information about the writing is gathered in order to complete a rough outline and a final outline.

Choose one of the following main topics:

- how to plant a seed in a garden
- how to build a snowman
- think of your own main topic

Write your main topic on the main topic section of the rough outline.

The entire outlining process is explained in **Appendix A**. If you need help in completing the rough outline or the final outline, use Appendix A. Whether or not you use Appendix A, you still need to complete the rough outline and the final outline on the next two pages of this lesson.

Complete the rough outline

## Rough Outline

**Main topic:** _____

**Detail #1:** _____

**Detail #2:** _____

**Detail #3:** _____

**Lesson 25 Day 2**

Date: _____

# How-to Paragraphs

Complete the final outline

## Final Outline

**Topic sentence:**
_____
_____
_____
_____

**Detail sentence #1:**
_____
_____
_____
_____

**Detail sentence #2:**
_____
_____
_____
_____

**Detail sentence #3:**
_____
_____
_____
_____

**Ending sentence:**
_____
_____
_____
_____

Level 3, Lesson 25 – How-to Paragraphs

**Lesson 25 Day 3**

# How-to Paragraphs

Date: _____

## Drafting Process

### Complete the rough draft

So far you have spent quite a bit of time filling out the rough outline and the final outline. As a result, your final outline has all of the necessary pieces to complete your writing.

If you think of something you want to add while you are writing your rough draft, please do so. The final outline will now be used as a guide to write a rough draft of the writing.

Start by writing your **topic sentence**, **detail sentences**, and **ending sentence** on the lines below.

_____
_____
_____
_____
_____
_____
_____
_____
_____
_____

**Lesson 25 Day 4**

Date: _____

## How-to Paragraphs

Edit the rough draft

It is now time to **edit** the rough draft you wrote on Day 3. Does your paragraph say what you want it to say? Do the words you chose make sense?

Look for and fix the following errors: 1) incorrectly used, misspelled, or misplaced words, 2) incorrect or missing spacing, 3) incorrect, missing, or misplaced punctuation, and 4) incorrect or missing capitalization.

**Lesson 25 Day 5**

Date: _____

# How-to Paragraphs

## Complete the final draft

On Day 4 you edited your paragraph. Today you will rewrite your paragraph in its final draft form.

Read your paragraph one more time. Do your sentences make sense? Are your sentences related enough to be in the same paragraph? Can you make it even better by adding 1) **transition words**, 2) **strong verbs**, 3) **adverbs**, 4) **exact nouns**, or 5) **descriptive adjectives**? Rewrite your edited paragraph below in its final form.

**Lesson 26 Day 1**

# Persuasive Paragraphs

Date: _____

In this lesson you will write a **persuasive paragraph**. A persuasive paragraph is one that tries to convince or persuade someone to do something, to believe in something, or to agree with the writer's opinion. Usually the writer gives several arguments which support his position.

Introductory Sentence: This is where the writer tells his audience what he is trying to convince them to agree with, believe in, or do.

Body of Paragraph (detail sentences): This is where the writer gives the details of his argument. These sentences should support and agree with the introductory sentence. The writer should use descriptive words (adjectives) to express his position.

Ending Sentence: The writer uses this sentence to summarize his arguments given in the body of the paragraph. The writer uses this sentence to make one last plea to the reader to try and persuade him.

### Why My Parents Should Buy Me a New Bicycle

I need a new bicycle because my bicycle is old and too small for me. First, my current bicycle is very old. In fact, it is much older than I am since it used to be my older brother's bicycle. Next, my bicycle is too small for me. Last summer Dad raised the seat as high as it could go and it was fine. Since last summer, I have grown several inches and now my knees hit my chest when I peddle. Finally, the chain keeps coming off when I peddle. Last year I caught a pair of my favorite pants in the chain and ruined them. I believe something is bent that keeps making the chain fall off. I need a new bicycle because my bike is very old, and it is really too small for me.

Develop and write a persuasive paragraph using the following writing process:

Outlining Process
   A. Choose a main topic
   A. Complete the rough outline
   B. Complete the final outline

Drafting process
   A. Complete the rough draft
   B. Edit the rough draft
   C. Complete the final draft

**Outlining Process**

We will now begin writing a persuasive paragraph with the outlining process. Outlining is the process where information about the writing is gathered in order to complete a rough outline and a final outline.

Choose from one of the following main topics:

- asking for a pet
- asking for a specific gift for your birthday
- going to your favorite restaurant
- think of your own main topic

Write your main topic on the main topic section of the rough outline.

The entire outlining process is explained in **Appendix A**. If you need help in completing the rough outline or the final outline, use Appendix A. Whether or not you use Appendix A, you still need to complete the rough outline and the final outline on the next two pages of this lesson.

Level 3, Lesson 26 – Persuasive Paragraphs

## Complete the rough outline

### Rough Outline

**Main topic:** _____

**Detail #1:** _____
_____
_____
_____

**Detail #2:** _____
_____
_____
_____

**Detail #3:** _____
_____
_____
_____

**Lesson 26 Day 2**

Date: _____

# Persuasive Paragraphs

Complete the final outline

## Final Outline

**Topic sentence:**
_____
_____
_____
_____

**Detail sentence #1:**
_____
_____
_____
_____

**Detail sentence #2:**
_____
_____
_____
_____

**Detail sentence #3:**
_____
_____
_____
_____

**Ending sentence:**
_____
_____
_____
_____

Level 3, Lesson 26 – Persuasive Paragraphs

**Lesson 26 Day 3**

Date: _____

# Persuasive Paragraphs

## Drafting Process

### Complete the rough draft

So far you have spent quite a bit of time filling out the rough outline and the final outline. As a result, your final outline has all of the necessary pieces to complete your writing.

If you think of something you want to add while you are writing your rough draft, please do so. The final outline will now be used as a guide to write a rough draft of the writing.

Start by writing your **topic sentence**, **detail sentences**, and **ending sentence** on the lines below.

_____
_____
_____
_____
_____
_____
_____
_____
_____
_____
_____
_____
_____
_____
_____

**Lesson 26 Day 4**

# Persuasive Paragraphs

Date: _____

## Edit the rough draft

It is now time to **edit** the rough draft you wrote on Day 3. Does your paragraph say what you want it to say? Do the words you chose make sense?

Look for and fix the following errors: 1) incorrectly used, misspelled, or misplaced words, 2) incorrect or missing spacing, 3) incorrect, missing, or misplaced punctuation, and 4) incorrect or missing capitalization.

Lesson 26 Day 5

Date: _____

# Persuasive Paragraphs

Complete the final draft

On Day 4 you edited your paragraph. Today you will rewrite your paragraph in its final draft form.

Read your paragraph one more time. Do your sentences make sense? Are your sentences related enough to be in the same paragraph? Can you make it even better by adding 1) **transition words**, 2) **strong verbs**, 3) **adverbs**, 4) **exact nouns**, or 5) **descriptive adjectives**? Rewrite your edited paragraph below in its final form.

_____
_____
_____
_____
_____
_____
_____
_____
_____
_____
_____
_____
_____
_____
_____
_____

Level 3, Lesson 26 – Persuasive Paragraphs

**Lesson 27 Day 1**

Date: _____

# Informational Paragraphs

In this lesson you will write an **informational paragraph**. An informational paragraph is one that tells **facts** about **one** topic. An informational paragraph does **not** include the writer's opinion or try to cover multiple topics. The goal of a good informational paragraph is to provide the reader only with factual information.

In order to make informational paragraphs more interesting, be sure to include **exciting adjectives** and **adverbs**. Here is an example of an informational paragraph.

### Lunar Facts

The moon is a fascinating celestial body. First, the beautiful moon is not a planet but is a satellite orbiting the earth. Second, the moon is only about one-fourth the size of the earth. Also, the earth rotates about 100 times faster than the moon. Lastly, from earth we always see the same side of the moon. The other side is always hidden from us here on earth. The moon is a fascinating place.

Develop and write an informational paragraph using the following writing process:

Outlining Process
    A. Choose a main topic
    B. Complete the rough outline
    C. Complete the final outline

Drafting Process
    A. Complete the rough draft
    B. Edit the rough draft
    C. Complete the final draft

## Outlining Process

We will now begin writing an informational paragraph with the outlining process. Outlining is the process where information about the writing is gathered in order to complete a rough outline and a final outline.

Choose from one of the following main topics:
- your favorite video game
- your favorite meal
- think of your own main topic

Write your main topic on the main topic section of the rough outline.

The entire outlining process is explained in **Appendix A**. If you need help in completing the rough outline or the final outline, use Appendix A. Whether or not you use Appendix A, you still need to complete the rough outline and the final outline on the next two pages of this lesson.

## Complete the rough outline

### Rough Outline

**Main topic:** _____

**Detail #1:** _____

**Detail #2:** _____

**Detail #3:** _____

**Lesson 27 Day 2**

Date: _____

# Informational Paragraphs

Complete the final outline

Final Outline

**Topic sentence:**
_____
_____
_____
_____

**Detail sentence #1:**
_____
_____
_____
_____

**Detail sentence #2:**
_____
_____
_____
_____

**Detail sentence #3:**
_____
_____
_____
_____

**Ending sentence:**
_____
_____
_____
_____

**Lesson 27 Day 3**

Date: _____

## Informational Paragraphs

**Drafting Process**

Complete the rough draft

So far you have spent quite a bit of time filling out the rough outline and the final outline. As a result, your final outline has all of the necessary pieces to complete your writing.

If you think of something you want to add while you are writing your rough draft, please do so. The final outline will now be used as a guide to write a rough draft of the writing.

Start by writing your **topic sentence**, **detail sentences**, and **ending sentence** on the lines below.

_____
------------------------------------------------
_____
_____
------------------------------------------------
_____
_____
------------------------------------------------
_____
_____
------------------------------------------------
_____
_____
------------------------------------------------
_____
_____
------------------------------------------------

**Lesson 27 Day 4**

Date: _____

## Informational Paragraphs

### Edit the rough draft

It is now time to **edit** the rough draft you wrote on Day 3. Does your paragraph say what you want it to say? Do the words you chose make sense?

Look for and fix the following errors: 1) incorrectly used, misspelled, or misplaced words, 2) incorrect or missing spacing, 3) incorrect, missing, or misplaced punctuation, and 4) incorrect or missing capitalization.

**Lesson 27 Day 5**

Date: _____

# Informational Paragraphs

## Complete the final draft

On Day 4 you edited your paragraph. Today you will rewrite your paragraph in its final draft form.

Read your paragraph one more time. Do your sentences make sense? Are your sentences related enough to be in the same paragraph? Can you make it even better by adding 1) **transition words**, 2) **strong verbs**, 3) **adverbs**, 4) **exact nouns**, or 5) **descriptive adjectives**? Rewrite your edited paragraph below in its final form.

_____
_____
_____
_____
_____
_____
_____
_____
_____
_____
_____
_____

Lesson 28 Day 1

Date: _____

# Compare and Contrast Paragraphs

In this lesson you will write a **compare and contrast paragraph**. This lesson is about **comparing** and **contrasting** things when we write. When we **compare** things we are identifying ways in which two or more things are **similar**.

For example, if we are **comparing** a football and a basketball, we might say that both are filled with air, both are thrown into the air, and both are made out of similar materials. When we **compare** things in a paragraph we need to give the reader clues that we are comparing. To do this we use words such as **alike**, **both**, **similar**, **likewise**, **the same as**, and **also**.

For example: **Both** an apple and a pear are types of fruit.

An apple and a pear have **similar** features like an outer skin.

In comparison, when we **contrast** two or more things we are identifying ways in which they are **different**. For example, if we were **contrasting** a football to a basketball, we would say that one has pointy ends and the other does not. One has lacing and the other does not. When we **contrast** things in a paragraph we need to give the reader clues that we are contrasting. To do this we use words such as **different**, **does not**, **but**, **in contrast**, **conversely**, **on the other hand**, **on the contrary**, and **however**.

For example: Tara likes to eat fish, **but** her sister does not.

Tara is **different** from her sister because she likes fish.

Level 3, Lesson 27 – Informational Paragraphs

Develop and write a compare and contrast paragraph using the following writing process:

Outlining Process
   A. Choose a main topic
   B. Complete the rough outline
   C. Complete the final outline

Drafting process
   A. Complete the rough draft
   B. Edit the rough draft
   C. Complete the final draft

**Outlining Process**

We will now begin writing a compare and contrast paragraph with the outlining process. Outlining is the process where information about the writing is gathered in order to complete a rough outline and a final outline.

Choose from one of the following main topics:

- two places you have visited
- two types of restaurants
- two types of sports

Write your main topic on the main topic section of the rough outline.

The entire outlining process is explained in **Appendix A**. If you need help in completing the rough outline or the final outline, use Appendix A. Whether or not you use Appendix A, you still need to complete the rough outline and the final outline on the next two pages of this lesson.

## Complete the rough outline

Rough Outline

**Main topic:** _____

**Detail #1:** _____
_____
_____
_____

**Detail #2:** _____
_____
_____
_____

**Detail #3:** _____
_____
_____
_____

Lesson 28
Day 2

# Compare and Contrast Paragraphs

Date: _____

Complete the final outline

Final Outline

**Topic sentence:**

**Detail sentence #1:**

**Detail sentence #2:**

**Detail sentence #3:**

**Ending sentence:**

**Lesson 28 Day 3**

Date: _____

## Compare and Contrast Paragraphs

### Drafting Process

Complete the rough draft

So far you have spent quite a bit of time filling out the rough outline and the final outline. As a result, your final outline has all of the necessary pieces to complete your writing.

If you think of something you want to add while you are writing your rough draft, please do so. The final outline will now be used as a guide to write a rough draft of the writing.

Start by writing your **topic sentence**, **detail sentences**, and **ending sentence** on the lines below.

**Lesson 28 Day 4**

Date: _____

# Compare and Contrast Paragraphs

<u>Edit the rough draft</u>

It is now time to **edit** the rough draft you wrote on Day 3. Does your paragraph say what you want it to say? Do the words you chose make sense?

Look for and fix the following errors: 1) incorrectly used, misspelled, or misplaced words, 2) incorrect or missing spacing, 3) incorrect, missing, or misplaced punctuation, and 4) incorrect or missing capitalization.

**Lesson 28 Day 5**

Date: _____

# Compare and Contrast Paragraphs

Complete the final draft

On Day 4 you edited your paragraph. Today you will rewrite your paragraph in its final draft form.

Read your paragraph one more time. Do your sentences make sense? Are your sentences related enough to be in the same paragraph? Can you make it even better by adding 1) **transition words**, 2) **strong verbs**, 3) **adverbs**, 4) **exact nouns**, or 5) **descriptive adjectives**? Rewrite your edited paragraph below in its final form.

**Lesson 29 Day 1**

Date: _____

# Writing Poems

In this lesson you will learn how to write a **poem**. A poem is kind of like a story that is arranged in phrases that may or may not rhyme. Sometimes it's hard to tell when you are reading a poem, but usually a poem either rhymes or has a rhythm when you read it. Here is a sample poem:

**"The Hat Lady"**
There once was an old lady who lived in a hat,
It was cramped in there because of a rat.
She was up to her brim in fear,
Because the rat tried to bite her ear.
She finally got rid of it with a broom,
And now she has much more room.

The style of the above poem is the kind we will write in this lesson. You can see that the ending word of each pair of lines rhymes. In this type of poem some lines are complete sentences and some are not. You will also notice that every other line ends with a period while the rest end with a comma.

A. Finish the pairs of phrases below with words that rhyme with the words in bold.

1. I was the guy who ran the **race**, _____

   Even though I did not get first _____.

2. Since I was the **winner**, _____

   I won a free _____.

Level 3, Lesson 29 – Writing Poems

3. The apple was as red as a **rose**,
   _____

   Julie could smell it with her _____.

4. Fred was two hours **late**,
   _____

   And he arrived on the wrong _____.

5. The boxer had to **sit**,
   _____

   After taking a hard _____.

6. Suzie was feeling sick in her **head**,
   _____

   So she took a long nap in her _____.

7. Martha was hungry and wanted to go to the **store**,
   _____

   She had some food but wanted _____.

8. Tom needed a ride and waited for the **bus**,
   _____

   Later we went by, and he got a ride from _____.

**Lesson 29 Day 2**

Date: _____

# Writing Poems

A. Finish the rhyme below with your own rhyming second phrase for each pair. Have fun with this one. There are no wrong answers, but make sure the last word in your lines rhyme with the last word on the lines given below.

1. It was just about time,
   _____
   _____.

2. My skin was dry from playing in the ocean,
   _____
   _____.

3. I have fun when I ride my bike,
   _____
   _____.

4. My brother and I like to play,
   _____
   _____.

5. It was Mike's turn to sit in the chair,
   _____
   _____.

6. Laura was waving to the large crowd,
   _____
   _____.

7. Mom and I wanted to go on a walk,
   _____
   _____.

8. I went to the doctor and he said I was ill,
   _____
   _____.

Level 3, Lesson 29 – Writing Poems

**Lesson 29 Day 3**

# Writing Poems

Date: _____

So far you have learned how to select words that rhyme with others. You have also written the second half of a pair of phrases that rhyme. Now it is time to write a short poem.

First, determine generally what you want to write about. What do you want your poem to say? This general thought can be used to create the title of your poem.

Rather than trying to write your poem all at once, sometimes it is easier to first think of an **ending** to your poem. For example, assume that we want to write a poem about a duck. We have decided that the poem should end with the duck quacking and flying away.

Here is a rough draft of our **ending** phrase.
"the duck just quacked and flew away."

Then we move to the beginning of the poem. How do we want it to start? We might want our poem to begin with a duck swimming around in a pond, because that's what ducks usually do.

Here is a rough draft of our **beginning** phrase.
"One day I saw a duck swimming around in a pond,"

Level 3, Lesson 29 – Writing Poems

All we have to do now is fill in the middle portion of the poem. We need to make sure that the last words in each pair of phrases rhyme with each other. Here is what we came up with:

"My Friend the Duck"

One day I saw a duck swimming around in a pond,
I threw it a piece of bread and we developed a bond.
I wanted to stay with the duck and play,
but instead it just quacked and flew away.

You will notice that the last phrase has been modified a bit from our original idea. Sometimes changes are necessary in order make the phrase fit in the poem.

You can write a poem about almost anything. Think about someone you know who is funny, or think of some type of animal that can be funny.

A. Write a general idea of what you want to write about on the line below.

B. How do you want your poem to end? Write your idea below.

C. How do you want your poem to begin? Write your idea below.

Level 3, Lesson 29 – Writing Poems

Lesson 29
Day 4

Date: _____

# Writing Poems

Write your idea for a title on the first line. Take your ideas from Day 3 and write them as sentences. Remember, the last word of the beginning phrase must rhyme with the last word of the second phrase. The last word of the third phrase must rhyme with the last word of the ending phrase.

A. (Title)

B. (Beginning phrase)

C. (Second and third phrases) - Middle Part

Must Rhyme

Must Rhyme

D. (Ending phrase)

Must Rhyme

Level 3, Lesson 29 – Writing Poems

**Lesson 29 Day 5**

Date: _____

## Writing Poems

Take another look at the poem you wrote on Day 4. Make sure that your poem makes sense to the reader. Does your poem say what you want it to say? If you are not satisfied with your poem from Day 4, make some changes to it and rewrite it below. On the other hand, if you are satisfied with it as it is already written, then write a different poem below.

A. (Title)
_____
_____

B. (Beginning phrase)
_____
_____
_____
_____
_____,  ← Must Rhyme

C. (Second and third phrases) - Middle Part
_____
_____
_____
_____  ← Must Rhyme
_____.
_____
_____
_____
_____
_____,  ← Must Rhyme

D. (Ending phrase)
_____
_____
_____
_____  ← Must Rhyme
_____.

Level 3, Lesson 29 – Writing Poems

**Lesson 30 Review Day 1**

**Review of How-to Paragraphs**

Date: _____

A. Write an <u>X</u> by the items below that should be considered before writing a topic for a **how-to paragraph**.

1.___ Is the main topic something interesting that people will want to read?

2.___ Who is the intended audience?

3.___ Is the main topic too funny?

B. Do the steps in a **how-to paragraph** need to be arranged in any specific order. Write an <u>X</u> by the correct answer.

___ Yes

___ No

C. What does a **how-to paragraph** tell the reader? Write an <u>X</u> by the correct answer.

1.___ how the writer feels

2.___ how to accomplish a task

3.___ the writer's convincing view about something

4.___ something that happened to the writer

5.___ it provides facts about one topic to the reader

6.___ how two things are different or the same

Level 3, Lesson 30 - Review of Lessons 25-29

**Lesson 30 Review Day 2**

# Review of Persuasive Paragraphs

Date: _____

A. What is an important item to look for when reviewing a rough draft of a **persuasive paragraph**? Write an **X** by the correct answers.

1. ___ Did the writer make arguments that were persuasive enough to get the readers to agree?

2. ___ Did the writer use enough **strong verbs** to make his position sound convincing?

3. ___ Did the writer use enough **periods** to break up longer sentences into many choppy sentences?

4. ___ Did the writer use enough **descriptive adjectives** in the paragraph that will help convince the reader?

5. ___ Is the paragraph worded appropriately for the intended audience?

B. What does a **persuasive paragraph** tell the reader? Write an **X** by the correct answer.

1. ___ how the writer feels

2. ___ how to accomplish a task

3. ___ the writer's convincing view about something

4. ___ something that happened to the writer

5. ___ it provides facts about one main topic to the reader

6. ___ how two things are different or the same

Level 3, Lesson 30 - Review of Lessons 25-29

Lesson 30 Review Day 3

# Review of Informational Paragraphs

Date: _____

A. What is an important item to look for when reviewing a rough draft of an **informational paragraph**? Write an **X** by the correct answers.

1. ___ Did the writer express his opinion clearly?

2. ___ Did the writer use enough periods to break up longer sentences into many choppy sentences?

3. ___ Did the writer use enough **strong adverbs** to describe how the facts occurred?

4. ___ Did the writer use enough **exciting adjectives** to describe facts?

5. ___ Are the sentences worded appropriately for the intended audience?

B. What does a **informational paragraph** tell the reader? Write an **X** by the correct answer.

1. ___ the writer's opinion on a main topic

2. ___ facts about one main topic

3. ___ the writer's convincing view about something

4. ___ something that happened to the writer

5. ___ how to accomplish a task

6. ___ how two things are different or the same

**Lesson 30 Review Day 4**

Date: _____

# Review of Compare and Contrast Paragraphs

A. What is an important item to look for when reviewing a rough draft of a **compare** and **contrast paragraph**? Write an **X** by the correct answers.

   1.___ Did the writer limit his facts to one main topic?

   2.___ Did the writer use enough **strong verbs** to compare and contrast?

   3.___ Did the writer provide clear steps how to accomplish the task?

   4.___ Did the writer use enough **exciting adjectives** in the paragraph that will help show the comparing and contrasting?

   5.___ Are the sentences worded appropriately for the intended audience?

B. What does a **compare** and **contrast paragraph** tell the reader? Write an **X** by the correct answer.

   1.___ the writer's opinion on a main topic

   2.___ facts about one main topic

   3.___ the writer's convincing view about something

   4.___ something that happened to the writer

   5.___ how to accomplish a task

   6.___ how two things are different or the same

Level 3, Lesson 30 - Review of Lessons 25-29

C. When we **compare** two or more things in writing, what are we trying to show the reader? Write an <u>X</u> by the correct answer.

1.____ how one thing is smaller than the other

2.____ how things are the same

3.____ how one thing is a different color from something else

4.____ how things are different

D. When we **contrast** two or more things in writing, what are we trying to show the reader? Write an <u>X</u> by the correct answer.

1.____ how two things have the same feel

2.____ how things are the same

3.____ how two things are both a certain color

4.____ how things are different

**Lesson 30 Review Day 5**

Date: _____

# Review of Writing Poems

A. Finish the below pairs of phrases that rhyme.

1. He lifted the cover and what did he see,

   A buzzing, angry honey _____.

2. We played on the beach all day,

   If there was only someplace near we could _____.

3. While we were camping we had a great scare,

   _____ bear.

4. Alice's sandals were so tight that they gave her the blues,

   _____ shoes.

5. The sweet, round apple was as red as a rose,

   Julie could easily smell it with her _____.

6. There once was a lady _____.

   _____
   _____

7. Write your own poem here.

   _____
   _____
   _____,
   _____

Level 3, Lesson 30 - Review of Lessons 25-29

**Lesson 31 Day 1**

Date: _____

## Friendly Letters

A **friendly letter** is one that you write to someone you feel friendly towards. It usually **shares information** that is more personal than would be included in a letter sent for business reasons. A friendly letter might share information with a friend or family member. A **friendly letter** has **five** parts. They are the **heading**, **greeting**, **body**, **closing**, and **signature**.

Let's start at the beginning and explain each part.

### Heading

The first part of a friendly letter is the **heading**. The **heading** is in the upper **right corner** of your letter and contains **your address** and the **date**.

Example:  300 Plumb Street
Dallas, TX 75201
February 29, 2008

Remember to place a **comma** between the **city** and **state**. Also, a **comma** belongs between the **date** and the **year**.

### Greeting

The second part of a friendly letter is the **greeting**. The **greeting** usually starts with the word **Dear** followed by the person's name. The greeting is followed by a **comma**.

Example:  **Dear** Steve,

A. Write an **X** next to the **heading** that is written correctly.

1. ____ 100 Elm Street
San Diego CA 91210
February 3, 2010

2. ____ 100 elm street
San Diego CA 91210
February 3, 2010

3. ____ 100 Elm Street
San Diego, CA 91210
February 3, 2010

4. ____ 100 Elm Street
San Diego, CA 91210
february 3, 2010

B. Write an **X** next to each **greeting** that is written correctly.

1. _____ Dear Uncle Mike,

2. _____ Dear Ted,

3. _____ Dear alfred,

4. _____ Dear senator johnson,

C. Write this **heading** correctly. Remember to use **capital letters** and **punctuation** where needed.

800 Oak street
Akron OH, 44301
june, 23 2011

---

Level 3, Lesson 31 – Friendly Letters

**Lesson 31 Day 2**

Date: _____

# Friendly Letters

On Day 1 of this lesson we learned about the **heading** and the **greeting** of a **friendly letter**. In this part of the lesson we will learn about the remaining three parts, which are the **body**, **closing**, and **signature**.

## Body

The **body** is the third part a **friendly letter**. The **body** includes the message you want to write. Each paragraph should be **indented** half an inch from the left margin of the paper.

**Example**:  I am so excited to tell you that I finally got a new puppy. His name is Brutus and he likes to play outside. He is only 12 weeks old and he can already play fetch. I cannot wait for you to see him the next time you visit.

## Closing

The **closing** is the fourth part of a **friendly letter** and is the way we say goodbye. Typically, the **closing** in a friendly letter uses words like **Yours truly**, **With love**, **Your friend**, or something similar after the **body of the letter**. The first word of the **closing** is capitalized and a **comma** is placed after the **closing**.

**Example**: Yours truly**,**

Level 3, Lesson 31 – Friendly Letters

# Signature

The **signature** is the fifth and last part of a friendly letter. This is simply the name of the letter writer. The **signature** is placed directly below the **closing**. The **signature** can be handwritten or typed. Below is an example of the closing and signature as they are written together.

**Example**: Yours truly,
Casey

A. Write an **X** next to each **closing** that is written correctly.

1. _____ Sincerely,  3. _____ Thanks,

2. _____ Your Friend  4. _____ Your, humble servant,


B. Write an **X** next to each **closing/signature** that is written correctly.

1. _____ Thanks,  3. _____ Amy,
     Anne          I appreciate it!

2. _____ Your Friend,  4. _____ Your cousin.
     Allen               Kristin

Level 3, Lesson 31 – Friendly Letters

**Lesson 31 Day 3**

Date: _____

# Friendly Letters

A. Write the letter on the correct line below for each part of this **friendly letter**.

| A=greeting | B=body | C=signature | D=heading | E=closing |

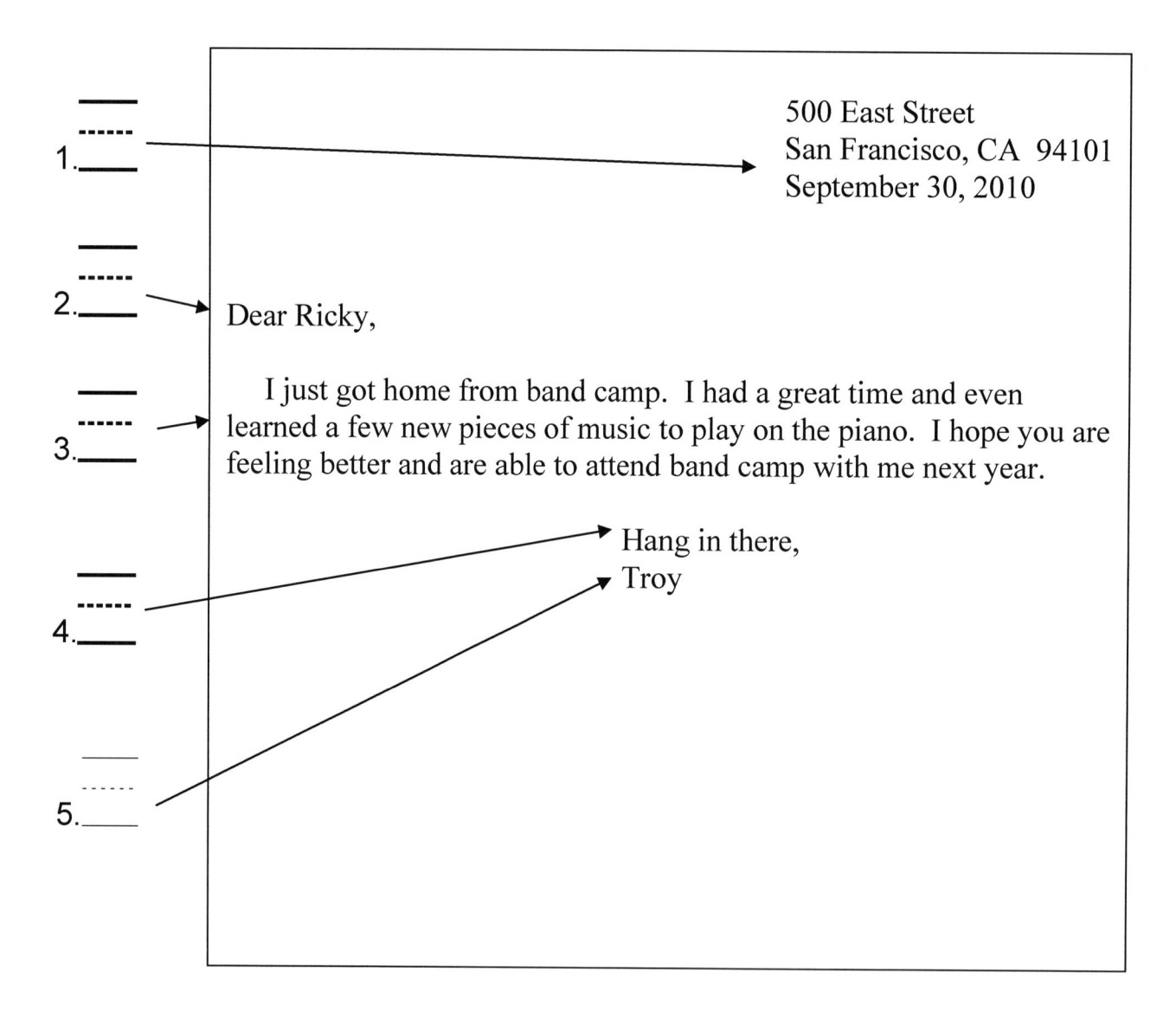

1. ____ → 500 East Street
San Francisco, CA 94101
September 30, 2010

2. ____ → Dear Ricky,

3. ____ → I just got home from band camp. I had a great time and even learned a few new pieces of music to play on the piano. I hope you are feeling better and are able to attend band camp with me next year.

4. ____ → Hang in there,

5. ____ → Troy

Level 3, Lesson 31 – Friendly Letters

Lesson 31
Day 4

Date: _____

# Friendly Letters

A. Write an **X** on the line for each correct answer.

1. Which part of a **friendly letter** greets the letter recipient?
    a. ___ heading
    b. ___ greeting
    c. ___ body
    d. ___ closing
    e. ___ signature

2. Which part of a **friendly letter** tells from whom the letter is sent?
    a. ___ heading
    b. ___ greeting
    c. ___ body
    d. ___ closing
    e. ___ signature

3. Which part of a **friendly letter** is the **main part**?
    a. ___ heading
    b. ___ greeting
    c. ___ body
    d. ___ closing
    e. ___ signature

4. Which part of a **friendly letter** says **goodbye**?
    a. ___ heading
    b. ___ greeting
    c. ___ body
    d. ___ closing
    e. ___ signature

Level 3, Lesson 31 – Friendly Letters

**Lesson 31 Day 5**

Date: _____

# Friendly Letters

When your **friendly letter** is finished you will need to mail it. Before the letter is mailed you will need to properly address an **envelope**.

An envelope has **two** addresses. The **first** is the address of the person **sending** the letter. This is written in the **upper left-hand** corner and is called the **return address**.

The **second** address is of the person **receiving** the letter. This is written in the **center** of the envelope and is called the **mailing address**.

**Example**:

```
Darren Evans
100 Main Street                                    [stamp]
Seattle WA 98101


                        Pete Avery
                        121 South 2nd Boulevard
                        Anytown MO 64108
```

The United States Postal Service suggests not using commas or periods when addressing an **envelope**. This is different from how we write a heading address for a friendly letter.

Finally, place a **stamp** in the upper **right-hand** corner. Your letter is now ready to be mailed.

Level 3, Lesson 31 – Friendly Letters

A. Write an __X__ next to the **envelope** that is written correctly.

1. \_\_\_\_\_

   Melanie Evercamp
   500 Camp Street
   Escanaba MI 49829

   Lane Myers
   Salt Lake City UT 84101

2. \_\_\_\_\_

   Melanie Evercamp
   500 Camp Street
   Escanaba MI 49829

   Lane Myers
   500 South Third Street
   Salt Lake City UT 84101

B. Address this **envelope**. Write the **sender's address** in the top left. Write the **receiver's address** in the center.

**Sender's Address**
Dan West
789 Prairie Street
Austin TX 78703

**Receiver's Address**
Bradley Johnson
566 Martin Drive
Ames IA 50010

Level 3, Lesson 31 – Friendly Letters

**Lesson 32 Day 1**

Date: _____

# Book Reports

A **book report** is something you write to let others know your opinion about a book you have read. This will help others decide whether they want to read the book.

Certain elements are always included in a book report. You should start with an **introduction**, which is a paragraph that includes the author's name and the title of the book. Book titles should be underlined. Also include a brief description of the type of book. Is it an adventure, fantasy, mystery, biography, fiction, or nonfiction story?

Next, write a paragraph providing some **details** of the book. Tell about the setting of the book. Where and when did it happen? Discuss the main characters and give a brief description of each one. Describe the plot briefly without giving too much information.

Finally, write a paragraph that includes your **opinion** of the book. This is the **conclusion**. Did you like it or dislike it? Provide reasons and examples.

### Example:

Daniels' Duck by Clyde Robert Bulla is a fiction book about a little boy named Daniel. He wants to be like a famous wood carver that he knows.

Daniel and his family live in Tennessee. They have a log cabin in the mountains. Daniel is a little boy who likes to carve wood. Henry Pettigrew is a wood-carver who carves animals. Daniel carved a duck and took it to the fair to sell.

I thought this was a nice book. I liked the part when Henry Pettigrew talked to Daniel about his duck. I would recommend this book to anyone who likes a happy ending.

A. Answer the following questions about the previous **book report**.

1. Write the title and author of the book.

2. Where does the story take place?

3. Who are the main characters in the story?

4. Write one or two sentences from the report that describe the book.

5. What is the writer's opinion of the book? Does the writer recommend the book?

Lesson 32
Day 2

Date: _____

# Book Reports

Here is another sample book report.

Hill of Fire by Thomas P. Lewis is a fiction book. It is about a village where things are the same every day.

The story takes place in a small village in Mexico. The farmer is a bored man because things are the same every day. Pablo is the farmer's son who helps him plow. One day something amazing happens that changes the village.

I liked this book because it was exciting to read. I felt sorry for the farmer when he was bored. I was scared for the village when they discovered the hill of fire. I would recommend this book to anyone who likes excitement.

A. Answer the following questions about the above **book report**.

1. Write the title and author of the book.

2. Where does the story take place?

3. Who are the main characters in the story?

Level 3, Lesson 32 – Book Reports

4. Write one or two sentences from the report that describe the book.

_____
_____
_____
_____
_____
_____

5. What is the writer's opinion of the book? Does the writer recommend the book?

_____
_____

Lesson 32 Day 3

Date: _____

# Book Reports

Here is another sample book report.

<u>Flat Stanley</u> by Jeff Brown is a fiction book about a boy from America who was made very thin by a bulletin board falling on him. He goes on fun adventures.

Stanley Lambchop is a young boy who is nice and friendly. He has a brother named Arthur. Stanley enjoys having fun and doing new things.

I thought this was a good book. I would recommend it to all of my friends. I am glad that I have this book and will read it again.

A. Answer the following questions about the above **book report**.

1. Write the title and author of the book.
   _____
   _____
   _____
   _____

2. Where does the story take place?
   _____
   _____

3. Who are the main characters in the story?
   _____
   _____
   _____
   _____

Level 3, Lesson 32 – Book Reports

4. Write one or two sentences from the report that describe the book.

5. What is the writer's opinion of the book? Does the writer recommend the book?

**Lesson 32 Day 4**

Date: _____

# Book Reports

Now it is your turn to write a book report for a book you have read recently. Remember to use all of the skills you have learned in previous lessons of this book for writing paragraphs. Also remember to include the following items in your **three** paragraph report.

1. Write the title and author of the book.
2. Where does the story take place?
3. Who are the main characters in the story?
4. Write one or two sentences that describe the book.
5. What is your opinion of the book? Do you recommend the book?

Level 3, Lesson 32 – Book Reports

**Lesson 32　Day 5**

Date: _____

## Book Reports

Write another book report. Remember to use all of the skills you have learned in previous lessons of this book for writing paragraphs. Also remember to include the following items in your **three** paragraph report.

1. Write the title and author of the book.
2. Where does the story take place?
3. Who are the main characters in the story?
4. Write one or two sentences that describe the book.
5. What is your opinion of the book? Do you recommend the book?

_____
_____
_____
_____
_____
_____
_____
_____
_____
_____
_____
_____
_____
_____
_____

Level 3, Lesson 32 – Book Reports

**Lesson 33 Day 1**

Date: _____

## Short Reports

You have already written an informational paragraph. In this lesson you will write **three** paragraphs. As you probably remember, an informational paragraph is one that contains information about a single topic. A **short report** is made up of more than one paragraph that are all related to the topic of the report.

Since a short report contains only facts and not the writer's opinion, the writer must find reliable facts wherever he can. This means the writer can look in books, interview witnesses, seek information from experts, observe facts, look on the Internet, read encyclopedias, find articles, read newspapers, and read magazines.

Information about outlining a short report is shown below.

**Title of the Report**

**Introductory Paragraph-** The topic sentence identifies the main topic for the short report. It also provides an explanation of why the report was written and a summary of its contents. The beginning paragraph also mentions the intention of the report, which is usually to provide information to help the reader make a decision about something.

**Informational Paragraph(s)**
Subtopic #1 (topic sentence)
- Detail #1 (used to make detail sentences)
- Detail #2 (used to make detail sentences)
- Detail #3 (used to make detail sentences)

May be more than one

**Concluding Paragraph-** The concluding paragraph acts as a summary for the entire short report.

Here is a short report that has two informational paragraphs.

1 ⟶ **"Wearing Mittens or Gloves"**

2 ⟶ This report explores the advantages of wearing mittens instead of gloves. It has been said that since mittens only have two compartments, one for the thumb and one for all of the fingers, they do not allow the wearer to use his hands when finger movement is needed. This report contains facts gathered from several places, including the Internet and other printed articles. The reader should find enough factual information here to make a decision whether it is better to wear gloves or mittens.

3 Mittens are clothing worn on the hands to keep the wearer's hands warm in very cold climates. Unlike gloves which have separate compartments for each finger, mittens only have two compartments, one for the fingers and one for the thumb. Although mittens do not allow for individual finger movement, most wearers say that they provide enough movement to perform all but the most difficult tasks. It is also well known that mittens are better at keeping the hands warm since the fingers touch each other and share body heat. Mittens are a great choice in the most severe climates.

Gloves are clothing worn on the hands that provide the wearer with separate finger movement since each finger has its own individual compartment. Gloves can be worn in all but the most severe cold conditions. With modern materials used to make gloves today, many wearers have found that they are preferred over mittens since they allow movement of each finger when a mitten does not. Gloves are very useful when the wearer needs to use each finger by itself.

4 ⟶ Gloves and mittens are both very useful in keeping the hands warm in cold climates. If the wearer needs separate movement of his fingers to perform tasks, gloves may be a great choice. On the other hand, mittens offer the most warmth when severe cold is present.

A. Go back and look at the previous short report. Label its parts below by using the items in the table.

| informational paragraphs | concluding paragraph | introductory paragraph | title of report |

1. _____

2. _____

3. _____

4. _____

**Lesson 33 Day 2**

Date: _____

## Short Reports

Think of something you would like to write a short report about. You can write about **your favorite planet**, **your favorite explorer**, **your home state**, or **think of your own main topic**.

For this **short report** you will only need **one** informational paragraph. In your informational paragraph you will have three details which will be turned into three or more detail sentences (on the final outline) for the informational paragraph.

Let's start the writing process by completing your rough outline. Write your **main topic** (report name) and **details** on the rough outline on the next page. Your details **will probably need to be investigated** in order to write your **short report**.

# Rough Outline

**Main topic**: _____

**Detail #1**: _____

**Detail #2**: _____

**Detail #3**: _____

**Lesson 33 Day 3**

Date: _____

## Short Reports

Use the information from your rough outline on Day 2 to complete the final outline for your informational paragraph. Do not worry if your sentences are not perfect or do not express your thoughts precisely.

### Final Outline

**Topic sentence:**
_____
_____
_____
_____
_____

**Detail sentence #1:**
_____
_____
_____
_____
_____

**Detail sentence #2:**
_____
_____
_____
_____
_____

**Detail sentence #3:**
_____
_____
_____
_____
_____

**Ending sentence:**
_____
_____
_____
_____
_____

Level 3, Lesson 33 – Short Reports

**Lesson 33 Day 4**

Date: _____

## Short Reports

Go back and read your **detail sentences** in the final outline. Do they say what you really want them to say? In your mind can you visualize how they will be linked together to build the informational paragraph for your short report?

You do **not** have to perform the **writing process** for the **introductory paragraph** or the **concluding paragraph** (we will learn how to do this next year in Winning With Writing - Level 4). Start building your report by writing an introductory paragraph, then build an informational paragraph from the final outline, and then write a concluding paragraph. Just do the best you can for the introductory and concluding paragraphs.

_____
_____
_____
_____
_____
_____
_____
_____
_____
_____
_____
_____
_____
_____
_____
_____
_____
_____
_____
_____
_____
_____

**Lesson 33 Day 5**

Date: _____

## Short Reports

Now it is time to write your **short report** in its final form. Go back and read the short report you wrote on Day 4. Do your sentences flow well from one to the other? Does your entire report provide helpful information to the reader? Make sure your sentences are properly capitalized and punctuated. Make some revisions to your short report to make it better. Write the final version on the lines below.

_____
_____
_____
_____
_____
_____
_____
_____
_____
_____
_____
_____

Level 3, Lesson 33 – Short Reports

**Lesson 34 Day 1**

Date: _____

# Biographies

In this lesson you will write a three paragraph **biography**. A biography is simply the story of someone's life. Biographies can be just a few sentences long, or they can fill an entire book. Biographies tell the basic facts about someone's life (living or dead) who is often famous or historical. Of course a biography can also be about ordinary people.

Biographies are typically written in chronological order, meaning they cover facts in order starting at an early point in a person's life and ending sometime later.

Biographers (the person writing the biography) use the following sources to find information: personal knowledge, writings, newspapers, other biographies, and articles to gather information about the person.

To find direction in writing a biography, the following steps should be taken:

1. Find basic facts about the person's life.
2. What parts of this person's life will you write about?
3. What questions would you want to ask this person?
4. What makes this person special or interesting?
5. What kind of effect did this person have on the world?
6. What events shaped or changed this person's life?
7. What obstacles did this person overcome?
8. Would the world be better or worse if this person hadn't been in it? How and why?

Level 3, Lesson 34 – Biographies

A. Think of someone you would like to write about. To make your assignment easier, write about someone you know so you can ask them for information.

   Write the person's name below.

   _____

B. Which parts of this person's life will you write about?

   _____

C. What question do you want to ask this person?

   _____

D. What makes this person special or interesting?

   _____

Level 3, Lesson 34 – Biographies

**Lesson 34 Day 2**

Date: _____

# Biographies

Let's continue with the biography that you started on Day 1.

A. What kind of effect did/does this person have on the world?

_____
_____
_____
_____

B. What events shaped or changed this person's life?

_____
_____
_____
_____

C. What obstacles did this person overcome?

_____
_____
_____
_____

D. Would the world be better or worse if this person hadn't been in it? How and why?

_____
_____
_____
_____

Level 3, Lesson 34 – Biographies

Lesson 34 Day 3

Date: _____

# Biographies

Normally, the writer would have to think of **details** to place in a rough outline, but since you have already gathered this information during Days 1 and 2 of this lesson, you can simply use that information to complete the final outline below (remember that all entries in a final outline must be complete sentences).

## Final Outline

- <u>Introductory Paragraph</u>:
  Who is this person?

  _____
  _____
  _____
  _____

  When was this person born?

  _____
  _____
  _____
  _____

  Why is this person special or interesting?

  _____
  _____
  _____
  _____

  What time period of this person's life will you cover?

  _____
  _____
  _____
  _____

Level 3, Lesson 34 – Biographies

- <u>Body Paragraph of Biography</u>:
  What kind of effect did this person have on the world?
  _____
  _____
  _____
  _____

  What events shaped or changed this person's life?
  _____
  _____
  _____
  _____

  What obstacles did this person overcome?
  _____
  _____
  _____
  _____

  Would the world be better or worse if this person hadn't been in it? How and why?
  _____
  _____
  _____
  _____

- <u>Concluding Paragraph</u>:
  This paragraph should summarize your biography.

Lesson 34
Day 4

# Biographies

Date: _____

We will now build a rough draft of your biography by writing the sentences you wrote from the final outline (Day 3) in order from top to bottom. Simply work your way down the final outline by writing the sentences you wrote in the introductory paragraph section, and then the sentences in the body of the paragraph. After you have written the introductory paragraph and body of your biography, write a concluding paragraph. The concluding paragraph simply acts as a short summary for your biography. Write a rough draft of your entire biography below.

Level 3, Lesson 34 – Biographies

**Lesson 34 Day 5**

Date: _____

# Biographies

Now it is time to write your **biography** in its final form. Go back and look at your rough draft from Day 4. Read it one more time. Do your sentences flow well from one to the other? Does your entire story make sense? Make sure your sentences are properly capitalized and punctuated. Write the final version of your biography on the lines below.

**Lesson 35 Day 1**

Date: _____

# Short Stories

In this lesson you will write a one paragraph **short creative story**. A short story is one where you get to use your imagination. You get to make up characters, places, and things that happen. Writing a short story should be the most enjoyable type of story to write since you do not have to do any research or ask anyone questions. All you have to do is use your imagination.

To find direction in writing a story, the following questions need to be answered:

1. What will the story be about? (main topic)
2. When and where does the story take place?
3. What happens in the story?
4. Who are the characters in the story?

Develop and write a short story paragraph using the following writing process:

Outlining Process
    A. Choose a main topic
    B. Complete the rough outline
    C. Complete the final outline

Drafting process
    A. Complete the rough draft
    B. Edit the rough draft
    C. Complete the final draft

**Outlining Process**

    We will now begin writing a short story with the outlining process. Outlining is the process where information about the writing is gathered in order to complete a rough outline and a final outline.

Choose one of the following main topics:

- a clown you saw at the circus
- a funny trick you would like to play on someone
- something you would like to do for fun

Write your main topic on the main topic section of the rough outline.

The entire outlining process is explained in **Appendix A**. If you need help in completing the rough outline or the final outline, use Appendix A. Whether or not you use Appendix A, you still need to complete the rough outline and the final outline on the next two pages of this lesson.

## Complete the rough outline

### Rough Outline

**Main topic:** _____

**Detail #1:** _____

**Detail #2:** _____

**Detail #3:** _____

**Lesson 35 Day 2**

Date: _____

# Short Stories

Complete the final outline

Final Outline

**Topic sentence:**
_____
_____
_____
_____

**Detail sentence #1:**
_____
_____
_____
_____

**Detail sentence #2:**
_____
_____
_____
_____

**Detail sentence #3:**
_____
_____
_____
_____

**Ending sentence:**
_____
_____
_____
_____

Level 3, Lesson 35 – Short Stories

**Lesson 35 Day 3**

Date: _____

## Short Stories

### Complete the rough draft

So far you have spent quite a bit of time filling out the rough outline and the final outline. As a result, your final outline has all of the necessary pieces to complete your writing.

If you think of something you want to add while you are writing your rough draft, please do so. The final outline will now be used as a guide to write a rough draft of the writing.

Start by writing your **topic sentence**, **detail sentences**, and **ending sentence** on the lines below.

**Lesson 35 Day 4**

Date: _____

## Short Stories

### Edit the rough draft

It is now time to **edit** the rough draft you wrote on Day 3. Does your paragraph say what you want it to say? Do the words you chose make sense?

Look for and fix the following errors: 1) incorrectly used, misspelled, or misplaced words, 2) incorrect or missing spacing, 3) incorrect, missing, or misplaced punctuation, and 4) incorrect or missing capitalization.

**Lesson 35 Day 5**

Date: _____

# Short Stories

## Complete the final draft

On Day 4 you edited your paragraph. Today you will rewrite your paragraph in its final draft form.

Read your paragraph one more time. Do your sentences make sense? Are your sentences related enough to be in the same paragraph? Can you make it even better by adding 1) **transition words**, 2) **strong verbs**, 3) **adverbs**, 4) **exact nouns**, or 5) **descriptive adjectives**? Rewrite your edited paragraph below in its final form.

**Lesson 36 Review Day 1**

Date: _____

## Review of Friendly Letters

A. Write an **X** next to the **heading** that is written correctly.

1. ____ 100 Union Road
   Glendale 91210 CA
   September 21, 2010

2. ____ 100 union road
   Glendale CA 91210
   September 21, 2010

3. ____ 100 Union Road
   Glendale, CA 91210
   september 21, 2010

4. ____ 100 Union Road
   Glendale, CA 91210
   September 21, 2010

B. Write an **X** next to each **greeting** that is written correctly.

1. _____ hi Ed,
2. _____ Dear Mom,
3. _____ Dear leslie
4. _____ Dear Sarah,

C. Write an **X** next to each **closing** that is written correctly.

1. _____ Later
2. _____ Your Friend,
3. _____ Thanks,
4. _____ Your, faithful son,

D. Write an **X** next to each **closing/signature** that is written correctly.

1. _____ Thanks,
   Jerry

2. _____ Your Friend.
   Allen

3. _____ Todd,
   I appreciate it!

4. _____ Your friend,
   Brian

Level 3, Lesson 36 - Review of Lessons 31-35

**Lesson 36 Review Day 2**

Date: _____

# Review of Book Reports

A. Write an **X** next to each answer that is correct.

1.____ A book report is a report that lets others know your opinion about a book you have read.

2.____ A book report helps others decide if they would like to read a certain book.

3.____ A book report lets the reader know the qualifications of the reviewer.

4.____ A book report tells the reader exactly what happened in the book, including the ending of the book.

B. What does a book report always contain? Write an **X** next to each answer that is correct.

1.____ an introduction

2.____ the authors name

3.____ how much the book weighs

4.____ title of the book

5.____ a conclusion

6.____ a complete description of what happens in the book

7.____ the reviewer's opinion of the book

8.____ a mention of the main characters

9.____ the entire plot is discussed

10.____ the type of book being reviewed (ex: mystery, fiction, non-fiction)

Level 3, Lesson 36 - Review of Lessons 31-35

**Lesson 36 Review Day 3**

Date: _____

# Review of Short Reports

Answer the following questions.

A. What is a short report? Write an **X** next the answer that is correct.

1. ___ It's a report of the weather for a given area.

2. ___ It helps others decide if they would like to read a certain book.

3. ___ It's a collection of informational paragraphs that all have different topics.

4. ___ It's a collection of informational paragraphs that all have a similar topic.

5. ___ It's a very small report that contains information about shorts and other types of clothing that are appropriate for the summer season.

B. Which is true about a short report? Write an **X** next to each answer that is correct.

1. ___ A short report can contain information from books.

2. ___ A short report can contain the writer's opinion.

3. ___ A short report can contain information from interviews of witnesses.

4. ___ A short report can contain information from magazines.

5. ___ A short report can contain information from an expert.

6. ___ A short report can contain information from the Internet.

7. ___ A short report can contain any information from encyclopedias.

Level 3, Lesson 36 - Review of Lessons 31-35

**Lesson 36 Review Day 4**

Date: _____

# Review of Biographies

A. Circle **true** or **false** for the following statements.

1. true or false    A biography is the story of someone's life.
2. true or false    A biography tells basic facts about someone's life.
3. true or false    A biography is only written about people who are living.
4. true or false    A biography is limited to 200 words.
5. true or false    A biography is usually written in chronological order.
6. true or false    A biography is written using only the writer's memory.

B. What kind of information goes into a biography? Write an **X** next to each answer that is correct.

1. ___ certain parts of this person's life
2. ___ information about the writer
3. ___ information that makes the person special or interesting
4. ___ the effect this person had on the world
5. ___ how long it took to write the biography
6. ___ events that shaped or changed this person's life
7. ___ obstacles that this person overcame

C. Biographers use which kinds of sources to find information? Write an **X** next to each answer that is correct.

1. ___ personal knowledge
2. ___ writings
3. ___ any type of information
4. ___ newspapers
5. ___ other biographies

Level 3, Lesson 36 - Review of Lessons 31-35

**Lesson 36 Review Day 5**

Date: _____

# Review of Short Stories

A. What is true about a short story? Write an **X** next to each answer that is correct.

1. ___ the writer gets to make up characters

2. ___ the writer does not use his imagination

3. ___ the writer does not need to tell where the story takes place

4. ___ the writer gets to make up the things that happen


B. Which items below are <u>always</u> part of a short story? Write an **X** next to each answer that is correct.

1. ___ a topic

2. ___ a plot

3. ___ characters

4. ___ animals

5. ___ a setting

6. ___ a beginning

7. ___ an ending

# Appendix A
# Outlining Process for a Single Paragraph

The **writing process** actually has two parts, the **outlining process** and the **drafting process**. The outlining process is the **act of gathering information** necessary to complete a **rough outline** and a **final outline**. This appendix will explain only the outlining process. The drafting process will be covered in each individual lesson where it is needed.

As mentioned above, there are two items that need to be completed during the outlining process, the rough outline and the final outline.

Complete the rough outline

The outlining process starts by completing the rough outline. After the rough outline is complete, the information it contains will be used to develop a final outline. The final outline will then be used as a guide to write a rough draft of the paragraph. Below is a sample rough outline that shows its parts.

Rough Outline

- Main Topic
    - Detail #1: (used to make detail sentences
    - Detail #2:   on the final outline)
    - Detail #3:

> May be more or fewer than three

*Step #1* (develop a main topic for the rough outline)

The first piece of information needed to complete the rough outline is a **main topic**. A main topic is a **very general idea** that tells what a paragraph is about. For example, let's assume we have decided that we want to write a paragraph about **arctic animals**. This bolded phrase is called the **main topic** of the paragraph. Notice that we called this a phrase and not a sentence. A main topic does not have to be a complete sentence. It only needs to be a very general **idea** for your paragraph.

A.  When you decide on a main topic, write it in the **main topic** section of your rough outline.

*Step #2* (develop details for the rough outline)

Now that we have a main topic (the sample is **arctic animals**), we need to think of **details** to complete the rough outline. A detail is a thought, phrase, or sentence that gives more information about the main topic. These details will be turned into **detail sentences** for the **final outline**.

Assume we possess no knowledge of our example main topic arctic animals, so we conducted some research to gather information from the library, Internet, and some other dependable sources. Our research returned the following **details** about arctic animals:

1. polar bears
2. seals
3. orcas

These are **details** because they provide more description to the main topic of **arctic animals**.

B.  Think of a few details for your main topic and write them under the **details** portion of the rough outline. With the addition of your **details**, the rough outline is complete.

Complete the final outline

The next step in organizing our paragraph is completing a final outline that has the following structure:

- Topic sentence:
- Detail Sentence #1: (constructed from the main
- Detail Sentence #2: topic and details in the
- Detail Sentence #3: rough outline)   — May be more or fewer than three
- Ending sentence:
    (restates the topic sentence and/or summarizes the detail sentences)

*Step #1* (write a topic sentence)

The first step to completing a final outline is writing a **topic sentence**. A topic sentence tells **generally** what the paragraph is about, but it does not provide specific detail about the paragraph. Its primary purpose is to get the attention of the reader.

By looking at the **main topic** and **details** written on the rough outline, we can use them to think of a **topic sentence** for the final outline. While the main topic in the rough outline may or may not be a complete sentence, the topic sentence in the final outline **must** be a complete sentence. Using our example main topic of **arctic animals**, our topic sentence could be something like the following sentence: **Arctic animals survive very well in the extreme cold**.

*Step #2* (writing detail sentences)

The next piece of information needed to build the final outline is detail sentences. Detail sentences will make up the greatest portion of your writing. They actually tell the story of the paragraph. This makes the detail sentences arguably the most important part of the writing.

Look at the **details** written on the rough outline. It is our goal to use these **details** along with the **main topic** and **topic sentence** to think of interesting detail sentences for the paragraph. While you are thinking of these **detail sentences**, remember that they will all need to fit together as a paragraph. By the time you are done you should have several detail sentences written under the **detail sentences** section of the final outline. Make sure to place the detail sentences in the correct order if there is a required order for your writing.

Since you now have all of the information you need to think of detail sentences, write your detail sentences in the detail sentences section of the final outline.

After looking at our details, main topic, and topic sentence from our example (arctic animals), we added some detail sentences to our final outline. Our final outline now looks like this:

## Final Outline

Topic Sentence:

   Arctic animals survive very well in the extreme cold.

Detail Sentences:

- Polar bears have a thick, furry coat which acts as a barrier to the cold.
- Seals have a thick layer of blubber and skin that protects them from the cold.
- Orcas can survive in cold water because they have a thick layer of blubber over their body.

Ending Sentence:

   (not developed yet)


*Step #3* (writing an ending sentence)

   The last step to completing the final outline is to create an **ending sentence**. It is the function of the ending sentence to restate the topic sentence or summarize the detail sentences. For our example above, we could write the following ending sentence:

   "As you can see, most arctic animals that survive the cold have blubber or some kind of insulation."

Create an ending sentence for your paragraph and write it on the **ending sentence** section of your final outline. With the addition of the ending sentence, your final outline is complete.